Contents

I Like Sizzling Sausages	John Foster	8
Landscape	Celia Warren	9
Plum, Peach, Pineapple, Pear	Mike Jubb	10
Little Jack Horner	Anon	11
Tastes	John Foster	12
Snow-cone	John Agard	13
Zelba Zinnamon	Sheree Fitch	14
Clumsy Clementina	Kaye Umansky	15
I Hate Spinach	Carolyn Graham	16
Poppadoms, Poppadoms	John Foster	17
Beans	Mike Jubb	18
Dad's Cooking Pancakes	John Foster	20
Bubblegum Balloon	Tony Mitton	22
Six Sweets	Wes Magee	23
Gingerbread Man	Celia Warren	24
A Munching Monster	Marian Swinger	26
When the Giant Comes to Breakfast	John Coldwell	27
Washing-Up	Wes Magee	28

I Like Sizzling Sausages

I like sizzling sausages.   I like bubbling beans.   I like cauliflower cheese
And all kinds of greens.

I like hot tomato soup.   I like chicken wings.   I like crisp fish fingers.
I like spaghetti rings.

I like eggs and bacon.   But most of all I really like
And Mum's potato cakes.   The fresh bread my gran bakes.

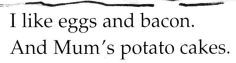

8   *John Foster*

Food Rhymes

Compiled by John Foster

Illustrated by Carol Thompson

Oxford University Press

Oxford   New York   Toronto

Oxford University Press, Great Clarendon Street, Oxford OX2 6DP

Oxford   New York
Athens Auckland Bangkok Bogota Bombay
Buenos Aires Calcutta Cape Town Dar es Salaam
Delhi Florence Hong Kong Istanbul Karachi
Kuala Lumpur Madras Madrid Melbourne
Mexico City Nairobi Paris Singapore
Taipei Tokyo Toronto Warsaw

and associated companies in
Berlin   Ibadan

Oxford is a trade mark of Oxford University Press

This selection and arrangement © John Foster 1998
Illustrations © Carol Thompson 1998
First published 1998

John Foster and Carol Thompson have asserted their moral
right to be identified as the authors of this work.

A CIP catalogue record for this book is available
from the British Library

ISBN 0 19 276165 X (paperback)
ISBN 0 19 276203 6 (hardback)

Printed in Belgium

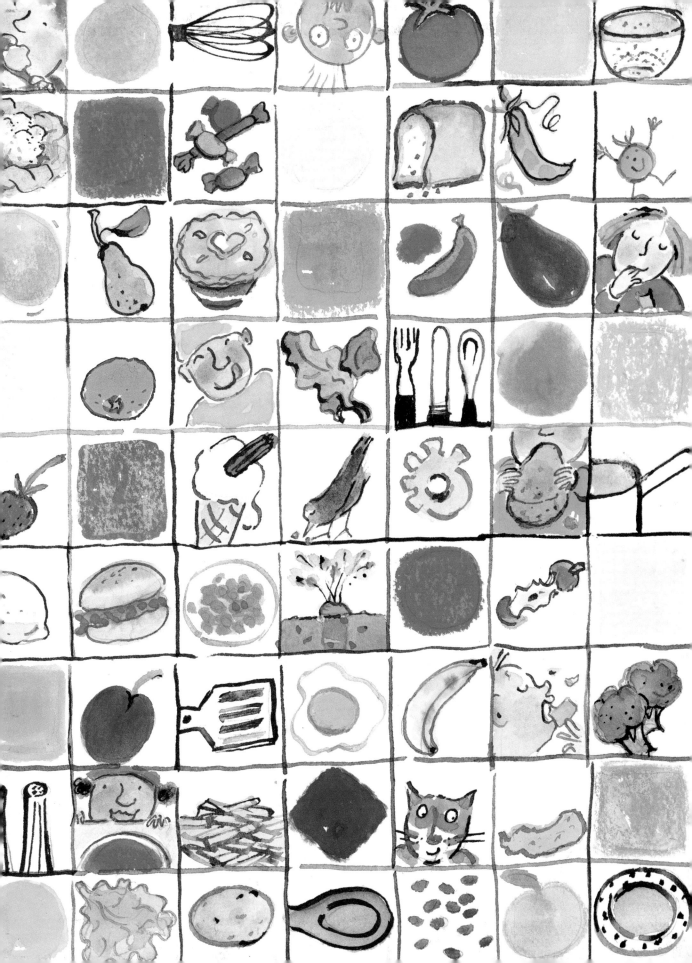

Landscape

My potato is an island.
The gravy is the sea.
The peas are people swimming;
The biggest one is me.

My carrots are whales
That make the sea wavy,
But the big brown blobs
Are LUMPS in the gravy!

Celia Warren

9

Plum, Peach, Pineapple, Pear

Plum, peach, pineapple, pear,
I could eat you anywhere;

Pear, plum, pineapple, peach,
Come for a picnic on the beach;

10

Peach, pear, pineapple, plum,
Hurry up and give me some!

Mike Jubb

Little Jack Horner

Little Jack Horner sat in a corner,
Eating his Christmas Pie.
He put in his thumb,
And pulled out a plum,
And squirted the juice in his eye.

Anon

11

Tastes

Jelly's slippery.

Ice-cream's cold.

Toffee's sweet
And sticky to hold.

Curry is hot
And full of spice.

Crisps are crunchy.

Chocolate's nice.

John Foster

Snow-cone

Snow-cone nice
snow-cone sweet
snow-cone is crush ice
and good for the heat.

When sun really hot
and I thirsty a lot,
me alone,
yes, me alone,
could eat ten snow-cone.

If you think is lie I tell
wait till you hear the snow-cone bell,
wait till you hear the snow-cone bell.

John Agard

13

Zelba Zinnamon

Zelba Zinnamon
She loved cinnamon
She loved cinnamon cake
Zelba Zinnamon
Ate so much cinnamon
She got a bellyache

Then Zelba Zinnamon
Sniffed the cinnamon
Got her nose all red
Zelba Zinnamon
Nose full of cinnamon
Had to go to bed.

Sheree Fitch

Clumsy Clementina

Clumsy Clementina
Tripped over the cat.
Up flew her ice cream,
Oops!
Bump!
Splat!
Cone in her ear,
Ice-cream on her clothes,
And a chocolate flake
Up
Her
Nose!

Kaye Umansky

15

I Hate Spinach

I hate spinach
I hate salt
I can't help it
It's not my fault.

I like sugar
I like tea
I like things that start with 'c'
Cookies, candy, chocolate cakes
I like the things that my mum bakes.

Carolyn Graham

Poppadoms, Poppadoms

Poppadoms, poppadoms,
with chicken and rice.
Poppadoms, poppadoms,
plain or spice.
Crispy hot poppadoms
to crunch and chew.
A plateful of poppadoms
for me and you.

John Foster

17

Beans

Beans on bread,
Beans on toast;
Beans are what I love the most.

Beans in a pie,
Beans in a stew;
Beans are what I love to chew.

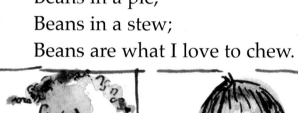

Beans and chips,
Beans and fish;
Beans are such a lovely dish.

Beans with veg,
Beans with meat;
Beans are what I want to eat.

I want beans!

Beans in a bun,
Beans in a roll,
Beans in a sandwich,
Beans in the hole,
Beans in a trifle,
Beans in a mousse,
Beans in lemonade,
Beans in juice,
Beans in a crumble,
Beans in a cake,
Beans in a cola,
Beans in a shake,
Beans with custard,
Beans with cream,
Give me beans, or I will SCREAM.

Mike Jubb

Dad's Cooking Pancakes

Dad's cooking pancakes for our tea—
One for you, one for you, and one for me.

Stir the batter in the bowl.
Mix.   Mix.   Mix.
Stir up all the flour and eggs.
Whisk.   Whisk.   Whisk.

Fry the batter in the pan.
Fry.   Fry.   Fry.
Toss the pancake in the air.
High.   High.   High.

Put the pancake on your plate,
Crisp and golden brown.
Sprinkle it with sugar
And gobble it down!

John Foster

21

Bubblegum Balloon

Bubblegum, bubblegum,
big pink balloon.

Bubblegum, bubblegum,
round like the moon.

Bubblegum, bubblegum,
planet in space.

Bubblegum bursting
in my face!

Tony Mitton

22

Six Sweets

Six sweets in a paper bag.
Shake them up and down.

Six sweets in a paper bag.
Shake them round and round.

RIP!

No sweets in a paper bag.
They're all on the ground!

Pick them up . . .

One
      Two
   Three
       Four
Five
   Six!

Wes Magee

23

Gingerbread Man

'Gingerbread's too hard,'
  said the Gingerbread Man,
'I'd rather be made of marzipan.'

'Marzipan's too soft,'
  said the Marzipan Man,
'I'd rather be made of strawberry jam.'

24

too runny

too stiff

'Strawberry jam's too runny,'
  said the Strawberry Jam Man,
'I'd rather be made of plain meringue.'

'Meringue's too stiff,'
  the Meringue Man said,
'I'd rather be made of gingerbread!'

Celia Warren

A Munching Monster

A monster ate a monster lunch,
a monster pie, a monster munch,
a monster apple, a monster plum.
The monster filled his monster tum.

He licked a monster lollipop.
He drank a bottle of monster pop.
He chomped a monster chocolate cake
and got a monster stomach ache.

Marian Swinger

26

When the Giant Comes to Breakfast

When the giant comes to breakfast,
He eats cornflakes with a spade,
Followed by a lorry-load
Of toast and marmalade.

Next, he takes a dustbin,
Fills it up with tea,
Drinks it all in a gulp
And leaves the mess for me.

John Coldwell

27

Washing-Up

Wash the spoons,
Wash the forks,
Wash each plate and cup.
Put your hands
In soapy suds
And do the washing-up.

Wash the pots,
Wash the pans,
Make them squeaky clean.
You're a splishy,
Splashy, sploshy
Washing-up machine!

Wes Magee

28

We are grateful to the following for permission to publish their poems for the first time in this collection:

John Foster: 'Dad's Cooking Pancakes', 'Tastes', and 'I like Sizzling Sausages', Copyright © John Foster 1998. **Carolyn Graham:** 'I Hate Spinach', Copyright © Carolyn Graham 1998. **Mike Jubb:** 'Plum, Peach, Pineapple, Pear' and 'Beans', both Copyright © Mike Jubb 1998. **Wes Magee:** 'Washing-up' and 'Six Sweets', both Copyright © Wes Magee 1998. **Tony Mitton:** 'Bubblegum Balloon', Copyright © Tony Mitton 1998. **Marian Swinger:** 'A Munching Monster', Copyright © Marian Swinger 1998. **Kaye Umansky:** 'Clumsy Clementina', Copyright © Kaye Umansky 1998, reprinted by permission of the author c/o Caroline Sheldon Literary Agency. **Celia Warren:** 'Landscape' and 'Gingerbread Man', both Copyright © Celia Warren 1998.

We also acknowledge permission to include previously published poems:

John Agard: 'Snow Cone' from *I Din Do Nuttin* by John Agard (Bodley Head, 1979), reprinted by permission of the author c/o Caroline Sheldon Literary Agency. **John Coldwell:** 'When the Giant Comes to Breakfast', Copyright © John Coldwell 1992, first published in *One in a Million* edited by Moira Andrews (Viking Kestrel, 1992), reprinted by permission of the author. **Sheree Fitch:** 'Zelba Zinnamon' from *Toes in My Nose*, Copyright © 1987 by Sheree Fitch, reprinted by permission of the publishers, Doubleday, Canada Ltd. **John Foster:** 'Poppadoms, Poppadoms', Copyright © John Foster 1991, first published in *Food Poems* (OUP, 1991), reprinted by permission of the author. While every effort has been made to trace and contact copyright holders, this has not always been possible. If contacted, the publisher will be pleased to correct any errors or omissions at the earliest opportunity.

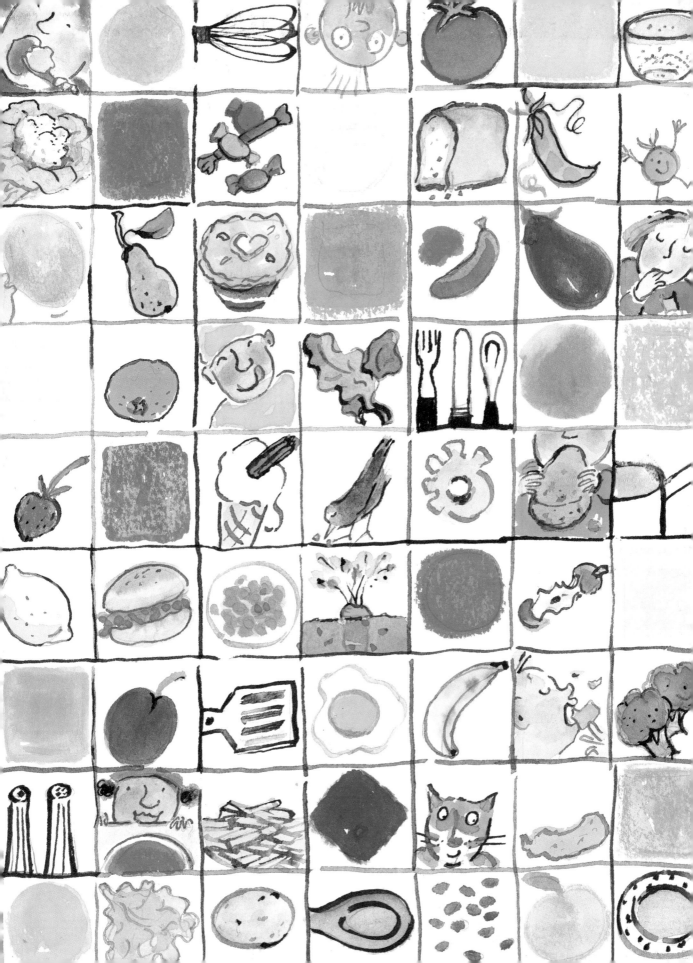